Speed up Your Way to Riches

Opening the Key to Enduring Thriving

By

Barr Randy M. Mixon

Table of contents

Introduction

Welcome to "Speed up Your Way to Riches: Opening the Key to Enduring Thriving." In this book, we set out on an extraordinary excursion to disentangle the secrets of abundance creation and find the keys to building persevering through flourishing.

We experience a daily reality such that monetary achievement is exceptionally pursued, yet few genuinely grasp the standards and techniques that lead to enduring riches. Numerous people spend their lives caught in a pattern of monetary vulnerability, battling to earn barely enough to get by and unfit to break liberated from the shackles of restricted assets. However, it doesn't need to be like this.

The way to abundance isn't exclusively saved for the fortunate few or the outstandingly skilled. It is a way that anybody can walk, equipped with the right information, outlook, and instruments. This book is your guide, your manual for exploring the unpredictable scene of abundance creation and revealing the secret fortunes inside.

All through these pages, we will dive into the mysteries that differentiate the people who thrive monetarily from the individuals who battle. We will investigate the force of outlook and how moving your convictions and viewpoints can open ways to overflow. We will inspect the significance of putting forth clear objectives, making compelling plans, and making a predictable move to carry your fantasies to completion.

Be that as it may, this book goes past simple hypotheses. It is a useful manual loaded up with noteworthy methodologies, down-to-earth activities, and genuine models that delineate the standards at play. Whether you are simply beginning your excursion to monetary autonomy or trying to upgrade your current riches, the experiences held inside these pages will assist you with speeding up your advancement and accomplishing enduring thriving.

We will investigate a great many points, including excelling at cash the board, utilizing the open doors in business and speculations, and fostering the propensities and disciplines that cultivate maintainable riches. We will likewise dig into the

Meaning of developing a development mentality, tackling the force of appreciation and perception, and making a steady organization of guides and similar people.

Moreover, this book perceives that abundance isn't restricted to financial overflow alone. Genuine thriving envelops all parts of our lives, including well-being, connections, and individual satisfaction. We will investigate the interconnectedness of these components and figure out how to adjust them amicably to make the existence of an all-encompassing overflow.

As we set out on this excursion together, I urge you to move toward these lessons with a receptive outlook and an eagerness to challenge your current convictions. The way to enduring flourishing requires a development-situated outlook and a pledge to persistent learning and improvement.

Is it true or not that you are prepared to open the key to enduring flourishing? Allow us to start our investigation of "Speed up Your Way to Abundance" and find the groundbreaking power that exists in you. Prepare to release your true capacity, conquer Monetary obstructions, and make an existence of overflow that will resound for a long time into the future.

Chapter 1

Grasping the Idea of Abundance

Understanding the idea of abundance goes past essentially connecting it with cash and assets. While monetary overflow is a piece of riches, genuine abundance envelops a lot more extensive and comprehensive viewpoint.

Abundance should be visible as a condition of flourishing that reaches out to different parts of life, including monetary dependability, close-to-home prosperity, satisfying connections, great well-being, self-awareness, and a feeling of direction. It is tied in with accomplishing an equilibrium and overflow in this multitude of regions.

To comprehend riches, it is essential to perceive that it isn't exclusively estimated by how much cash one has. Genuine abundance lies in having the assets and capacities to carry on with a satisfying and significant life, as well as the opportunity to seek after one's interests and objectives.

Abundance likewise includes developing a mentality that supports its fulfillment. This implies moving from a worldview limited by fear, which centers around need and limits, to an overflow outlook that perceives the boundless potential outcomes and open doors accessible. It includes having faith in one's capacity to make and draw in overflow in all everyday issues.

Besides, abundance isn't an objective yet an excursion. It is a ceaseless course of development, learning, and advancement. It requires progressing exertion, astute monetary administration, and the capacity to adjust to evolving conditions.

Eventually, understanding the idea of abundance includes perceiving that it goes past simple material belongings. It includes a comprehensive way to deal with life, zeroing in on generally speaking prosperity, self-improvement, and making a positive effect on oneself as well as other people. By embracing this more extensive comprehension, people can open the key to enduring thriving, and carrying on with a well-off and satisfying life.

Characterizing Riches: Past Cash and Assets

Characterizing abundance goes past the conventional comprehension of cash and assets. While these are frequently connected with riches, they are only one part of it. Genuine abundance envelops a more extensive and more all-encompassing point of view.

Abundance should be visible as the overflow and satisfaction in different everyday issues, including monetary, profound, physical, and otherworldly prosperity. It is tied in with having the assets and capacities to carry on with a significant and satisfying life.

Past cash and assets, abundance can include:

Wellbeing and Prosperity: Having great physical and emotional well-being is important. It permits you to appreciate life, seek after your objectives, and have the energy and essentialness to take part in significant exercises.

Connections and Associations: Significant connections and social associations contribute

Fundamentally to our prosperity. Having a steady organization of family, companions, and partners enhances our lives and offers close-to-home help.

Self-improvement: Abundance includes self-improvement and constant learning. Growing your insight, obtaining new abilities, and fostering your gifts add to your general abundance by opening up open doors and improving your confidence.

Time Opportunity: Having command throughout your time and the capacity to spend it on exercises that give you pleasure and satisfaction is a type of riches. Adjusting work, recreation, and special goals considers a balanced and fulfilling life.

Reason and Satisfaction: Genuine abundance lies in having a feeling of direction and importance throughout everyday life. Taking part in exercises that line up with your qualities and interests brings a profound feeling of satisfaction and fulfillment.

At last, characterizing abundance past cash and assets implies perceiving that material abundance alone doesn't ensure bliss and satisfaction. It includes developing a balanced and healthy lifestyle,

Where you have the assets, valuable open doors, and fulfillment in various parts of your life.

The Mentality of Abundance: Moving Your Point of View

The mentality of abundance alludes to how you think and see cash, overflow, and flourishing. It includes moving your point of view from a viewpoint that everything is limited to an overflow outlook.

A viewpoint that everything is limited is portrayed by a feeling of dread toward need and a conviction that there is restricted riches and opportunity accessible. Individuals with a worldview limited by fear will generally zero in on what they don't have and feel a consistent insecurity. This mentality can keep you away from facing challenges, chasing after valuable open doors, and pursuing sound monetary choices.

Then again, an overflow outlook is established in the conviction that there are a lot of riches and the chance to go around. A mentality perceives and

Values the overflow in your life, including monetary assets as well as connections, information, and encounters. With an overflow outlook, you view mishaps and difficulties as any open doors for development and learning.

Moving your point of view to a mentality of abundance includes a few key components:

Positive Reasoning: Taking on an inspirational perspective and zeroing in on conceivable outcomes as opposed to restrictions. This includes rethinking negative considerations and convictions about cash and overflow.

Appreciation: Rehearsing appreciation for what you have and recognizing the overflow in your life. By valuing the current second and remembering your good fortune, you make a positive starting point for drawing in more overflow.

Faith in Overflow: Fostering areas of strength for that there is sufficient riches and opportunity accessible for everybody. This conviction permits you to move toward monetary choices and potentially open doors with certainty and idealism.

Embracing Development and Picking up: Perceiving that self-improvement and learning are fundamental for accomplishing enduring thriving. Embracing consistent getting the hang of, searching out new information and abilities, and being available to new encounters can assist you with extending your growing substantial financial foundation potential.

Assuming Liability: Taking responsibility for monetary circumstances and understanding that you influence to make riches. This includes settling on proactive decisions, putting forth objectives, and making a reliable move towards making monetary progress.

By moving your point of view to a mentality of riches, you free yourself up to additional opportunities, draw in sure open doors, and go with enabled monetary choices. It permits you to beat restricting convictions and change your relationship with cash, eventually speeding up your way to enduring flourishing.

Chapter 2

The Job of Abundance in Accomplishing Enduring Success

The job of Abundance in Accomplishing Enduring Success

Abundance assumes a critical part in accomplishing enduring flourishing, yet it's essential to comprehend that abundance reaches out past financial belongings. Enduring thriving incorporates a comprehensive way to deal with prosperity, including monetary steadiness, individual satisfaction, and a feeling that everything is good.

Monetary dependability is a central part of enduring flourishing. Abundance gives us the necessary resources to meet our fundamental requirements and live serenely, without continually stressing over monetary weakness. It permits us to have a security net during crises and surprising occasions, giving a feeling of harmony and strength in our lives.

In addition, abundance offers amazing open doors for self-improvement and self-satisfaction. It

Empowers us to seek after our interests, put resources into schooling, and investigate new encounters. With monetary assets available to us, we Can grow our insight, gain new abilities, and seek pioneering adventures. This improves our self-awareness as well as opens ways to extra revenue sources and expert achievement.

The abundance additionally gives the opportunity and adaptability to settle on decisions lined up with our qualities and long-haul objectives. It permits us to have more command over our lives, whether it's choosing where to take up residence, how to invest our energy, or supporting causes we put stock in. This feeling of independence adds to our general prosperity and fulfillment.

Moreover, abundance can be a device for having a constructive outcome on the planet. At the point when we have an overflow, we can reward our networks, support admirable missions, and add to everyone's benefit. By utilizing our riches, we can make a gradually expanding influence of positive change and leave an enduring heritage that stretches out past our own lives.

In any case, it's vital to take note that abundance alone doesn't ensure enduring thriving. It is the dependable and deliberate administration of Abundance that prompts reasonable flourishing. This includes fostering an abundance mentality, pursuing shrewd monetary choices, rehearsing discipline, and embracing long-lasting learning. Making a reasonable way to deal with abundance lines up with our qualities, focuses on long-haul development, and considers the prosperity of ourselves as well as other people.

In synopsis, abundance assumes a significant part in accomplishing enduring success by giving monetary strength, opening doors for self-awareness, the opportunity for decision, and the capacity to have a beneficial outcome. When overseen carefully and with a more extensive viewpoint, abundance can add to a satisfying and prosperous life that goes past simple monetary achievement.

Explaining Your Monetary Objectives is a course of plainly recognizing and characterizing what you need to accomplish with your cash and monetary assets. It includes setting explicit goals that line up

With your qualities, needs, and long-haul yearnings. Here is a straightforward clarification of this idea:

Significance of Monetary Objectives: Monetary objectives give an internal compass and inspiration for your cash. They assist you with focusing on your spending, saving, and venture choices, guaranteeing that your monetary assets pursue issues most to you.

Distinguishing Your Qualities and Needs: Begin by pondering the main thing to you throughout everyday life. Think about your qualities, like family, security, self-improvement, or encounters. Contemplate your needs, such as purchasing a home, putting something aside for schooling, beginning a business, or accomplishing monetary freedom.

Defining Brilliant Objectives: Shrewd is an abbreviation for Explicit, Quantifiable, Feasible, Pertinent, and Time-bound. While laying out monetary objectives, ensure they are clear-cut, quantifiable, sensible, pertinent to your general vision, and have a particular period for the finish. For instance, rather than saying, "I need to set aside cash," a Brilliant objective could be, "I need to save

$10,000 within the following two years for an initial installment on a house."

Adjusting Objectives to Your Vision: Your monetary objectives ought to line up with your more extensive vision of enduring thriving and the existence you need to make. Consider how accomplishing these objectives will add to your general prosperity, bliss, and monetary security.

Separating Objectives into Noteworthy Stages: Whenever you have characterized your monetary objectives, separate them into more modest, reasonable errands. This assists you with making a significant arrangement and keeping tabs on your development en route. For example, on the off chance that you want to take care of your Visa obligation, you can separate it into regularly scheduled installment targets or investigate obligation solidification choices.

Normal Audit and Change: Monetary objectives are yet to be determined. Life conditions and needs can change, so it's vital to intermittently survey and change your objectives. Consistently evaluate whether your objectives are as yet applicable and

Make any essential alterations to keep them lined up with your advancing necessities and yearnings.

By explaining your monetary objectives, you gain lucidity and concentration, making it more straightforward to settle on informed monetary choices and do whatever it takes to accomplish enduring success.

Recognizing Your Qualities and Needs

Recognizing your qualities and needs is tied in with finding and explaining the main thing to you throughout everyday life. It includes figuring out your standards, convictions, and the regions that hold importance and significance for you. Concerning monetary objectives and growing a strong financial foundation, recognizing your qualities and needs is pivotal because it assists you adjust your activities and choices to what you really esteem.

Here is a straightforward clarification of the interaction:

Consider your life: Get some margin to ponder the various parts of your life, like connections, vocation, Self-awareness, well-being, and local area contribution. Consider what gives you pleasure, satisfaction, and a feeling of direction.

Focus on your qualities: When you have thought of the different perspectives that make a difference to you, focus on them in light of their significance. Contemplate which values are fundamental for your general prosperity and long-haul joy.

Think about the monetary ramifications: Presently, ponder how your qualities and needs connect with your monetary objectives. For instance, assuming family and quality time are vital to you, it very well may be essential to designate assets for getaways or exercises that reinforce family bonds. If self-awareness is fundamentally important, putting resources into schooling or expert improvement may be a savvy decision.

Survey what is happening: Assess your ongoing monetary standing, including pay, costs, investment funds, and obligations. This appraisal will assist you with adjusting your monetary assets to your qualities and focus on them in like manner.

Settle on purposeful choices: Equipped with an unmistakable comprehension of your qualities and needs, you can come to deliberate conclusions about how you dispense your monetary assets. This could include changing your ways of managing money, setting reserve funds targets, or putting resources into regions that line up with your qualities.

Audit and adjust: Consistently survey and reconsider your qualities and needs as they might develop over the long haul. As conditions change, you might have to make acclimations to guarantee your monetary objectives stay by what you genuinely esteem.

By recognizing your qualities and needs, you can adjust your monetary decisions to your desires, prompting a seriously satisfying and reason-driven way to deal with establishing long-term financial stability.

Laying out Brilliant Monetary Objectives

Laying out Brilliant monetary objectives is a strategy for laying out clear and significant goals to direct your monetary preparation and navigation. The abbreviation Savvy represents Explicit, Quantifiable, Feasible, Pertinent, and Time-bound. How about we separate every part:

Explicit: A Brilliant monetary objective ought to be characterized and centered. Rather than laying out an overall objective like "set aside cash," make it more unambiguous, for example, "save $5,000 for an upfront installment on a house."

Quantifiable: Your monetary objective ought to be quantifiable, permitting you to keep tabs on your development. For instance, assuming you want to take care of obligation, determine the specific sum you need to kill, similar to "pay off $10,000 in charge card obligation."

Feasible: Guarantee that your monetary objective is practical and achievable. Think about your ongoing monetary circumstance, pay, and costs. Laying out a ridiculous objective can prompt dissatisfaction and

Debilitation. Setting more modest achievements that lead to a bigger objective after some time is better.

Pertinent: Your monetary objective ought to line up with your more extensive monetary goals and needs. Inquire as to whether the objection applies to your by and large monetary prosperity. For example, on the off chance that your drawn-out objective is to begin a business, an important momentary objective May be to save a specific sum for introductory capital.

Time-bound: A Savvy monetary objective ought to have a particular period for fulfillment. Laying out a cutoff time makes a need to get going and assists you with keeping on track. Rather than saying "Set aside cash," put down a point in time bound objective like "save $1,000 in a half year."

By following the Shrewd system, you change dubious yearnings into substantial goals that are simpler to plan and pursue. Make sure to routinely audit and change your objectives on a case-by-case basis to remain focused and adjust to evolving conditions.

Making a Dream for Enduring Flourishing

Making a dream for enduring flourishing includes imagining the future you want concerning monetary overflow, security, and generally speaking prosperity. It goes past putting forth unambiguous monetary objectives and spotlights on making an Extensive and rousing image of what riches and flourishing mean to you.

To make a dream for enduring success, you want to make the accompanying strides:

Consider your qualities and needs: Begin by understanding the main thing to you. Think about your qualities, goals, and the way of life you need to lead. Recognize the components that add to your general feeling of satisfaction and bliss.

Envision your optimal future: Shut your eyes and envision the everyday routine you need to experience. Imagine yourself getting a charge out of independence from the rat race, having harmony of the psyche, and accomplishing your objectives. Envision the particular parts of your life that connote enduring thriving, like an agreeable home,

Satisfying connections, travel potential open doors, or the capacity to help causes you to care about.

Characterize accomplishment based on your conditions: Reject outer meanings of progress and make your own. Distinguish the particular achievements and accomplishments that connote Success to you. These could incorporate arriving at a specific degree of monetary freedom, constructing a flourishing business, or having the opportunity to seek after your interests without monetary imperatives.

Put forth aggressive yet sensible objectives: Separate your vision into significant objectives. Characterize both present moment and long haul goals that line up with your vision for enduring thriving. Guarantee these objectives are testing yet feasible, permitting you to extend past your ongoing constraints and develop.

Record your vision explanation: Articulate your vision for enduring flourishing in a succinct and strong proclamation. Utilize positive language, current state, and explicit subtleties to make it clear and convincing. Your vision explanation ought to act As a steady wake-up call of what you're pursuing and motivate you to make a reliable move.

Survey and update routinely: Return to your vision proclamation intermittently to guarantee it reverberates with your developing goals. As you develop and advance, your vision might develop as Well. Be available to refine and change it on a case-by-case basis.

Making a dream for enduring thriving gives you an unmistakable course and a feeling of direction. It adjusts your activities, choices, and every day propensities with your drawn-out objectives. By remembering your vision and making steady strides towards it, you increment your possibilities achieving enduring thriving and carrying on with a satisfying and bountiful life.

Chapter 3

Developing an Abundance Mentality

Developing an abundance mentality includes fostering a bunch of perspectives, convictions, and thought designs that help and draw in monetary overflow. It is tied in with taking on a positive and enabled outlook towards cash, riches, and flourishing. Here is a straightforward comprehension clarification of developing an abundance outlook:

Defeating Restricting Convictions: Perhaps the earliest move toward developing an abundance outlook is distinguishing and testing any restricting convictions you might have about cash. These convictions could be profoundly imbued and may incorporate thoughts like "cash is malevolent" or "I won't ever be rich." By perceiving these convictions and supplanting them with more certain and enabling ones, for example, "cash is a device for making a superior life" or "I'm fit for making monetary progress," you free yourself up to more prominent open doors.

Creating Overflow Cognizance: Overflow awareness is the conviction that there is a limitless stockpile of abundance and assets accessible to you. It includes moving your concentration from shortage and needs to overflow and probability. This attitude permits you to see open doors and opportunities for monetary development and achievement, instead of harping on restrictions and shortages.

Rehearsing Appreciation and Energy: Appreciation assumes an urgent part in developing an abundance outlook. By offering thanks for the cash and assets you right now have, you make a positive and Plentiful energy around your funds. This energy draws in additional riches and overflows into your life. Consistently recognizing and valuing the monetary endowments in your day-to-day existence assists with moving your mentality from a position of need to a position of overflow.

Embracing Learning and Development: An abundance outlook is likewise about continually looking for information and working on your monetary proficiency. It includes a readiness to gain from other people who have made monetary progress and to put resources into your very own

Monetary development. By persistently extending your insight and abilities in regions like money management, planning, and cash the board, you position yourself for long-haul monetary achievement.

Pursuing Activity and Embracing Open Doors: Developing an abundance outlook isn't just about certain reasoning; it likewise requires making a move. It includes effectively looking for and embracing valuable chances to develop your riches, whether it's through putting resources into resources, beginning a business, or chasing after professional Successes. An abundance mentality persuades you to go ahead with reasonable plans of action, get out of your usual range of familiarity, and jump all over chances that line up with your monetary objectives.

In outline, developing an abundance mentality includes perceiving and conquering restricting convictions, embracing overflow cognizance, rehearsing appreciation and energy, looking for information and development, and making a move to profit by opening doors. By fostering this mentality, you make areas of strength for drawing in

And creating enduring financial well-being and flourishing in your life.

Conquering Restricting Convictions about Cash

Conquering restricting convictions about cash includes testing and changing the negative or prohibitive contemplations and convictions we hold concerning our capacity to make and draw in abundance. These convictions frequently come from our childhood, social impacts, previous encounters, or cultural molding.

To get it and defeated restricting convictions about cash, it's fundamental to perceive and address normal negative convictions, for example,

"Cash is the base of all shrewd": This conviction proposes that cash itself is intrinsically terrible or adulterating. Nonetheless, cash is just an instrument that can be utilized for both positive and negative purposes. By moving this conviction, we can see cash as a way to set out open doors, have a beneficial outcome, and carry on with a satisfying life.

"I'm not meriting riches": This conviction spins around feeling dishonorable or undeserving of monetary overflow. It might come from sensations of low self-esteem or responsibility around cash. Perceiving and testing this conviction assists us with the understanding that everybody can make abundance and appreciate monetary achievement.

"Cash is scant and rare": This conviction expects that there is a restricted measure of cash accessible and that it is challenging to secure. In any case, by taking on an overflow outlook, we perceive that there are vast open doors and assets accessible to Make riches. Moving our point of view can open ways to additional opportunities and draw more overflow into our lives.

"I'm bad with cash": This conviction frequently emerges from past monetary errors or an absence of monetary training. It prompts an absence of trust in overseeing cash successfully. By looking for information, creating monetary abilities, and embracing solid cash propensities, we can supplant this conviction with the comprehension that monetary skills can be acquired and developed.

To beat these restricting convictions, it's vital to challenge them with positive certifications, perception methods, and rethinking methodologies. Encircling ourselves with steady and similar people who have a solid relationship with cash can likewise be helpful. Furthermore, looking for proficient direction from monetary counsels or mentors can give significant bits of knowledge and systems to reshape our attitude and ways of behaving around cash.

Keep in mind, conquering restricting convictions about cash is a slow cycle that requires mindfulness, Deliberate exertion, and reliable practice. Thusly, we can make a seriously enabling and bountiful relationship with cash, opening ways to enduring success and monetary prosperity.

Creating Overflow Cognizance

Creating overflow cognizance alludes to taking on a mentality and conviction framework that spotlights the overflow and limitless conceivable outcomes accessible throughout everyday life. It is tied in with moving your point of view from a world view

Limited by fear, where you accept that there is a restricted measure of assets and valuable open doors, to an overflow outlook, where you perceive the overflow and potential for development in different parts of life, including riches, achievement, connections, and individual satisfaction.

At the point when you foster overflow cognizance, you train your psyche to see open doors, conceivable outcomes, and arrangements as opposed to harping on restrictions and need. You begin to accept that there is enough for everybody and that your prosperity doesn't come to the detriment of others. This attitude engages you to think inventively, go ahead with reasonable plans of action, and immediately jump all over chances that come in your direction.

Here are a few vital standards and practices related to creating overflow cognizance:

Appreciation: Developing a feeling of appreciation for what you now have makes an uplifting perspective and draws additional good encounters into your life. By zeroing in on what you appreciate

And are thankful for, you shift your consideration away from shortage and need.

Positive Certifications: Utilizing positive assertions overhauls your psyche mind with engaging convictions. By rehashing proclamations like "I'm bountiful," "I draw in riches and potentially open doors," or "I merit achievement," you build up certain convictions and adjust your contemplations to overflow.

Perception: Picturing yourself previously encountering the overflow you want helps manifest it into the real world. By distinctively envisioning Yourself accomplishing your objectives and carrying on with a prosperous life, you make a psychological picture that initiates your psyche brain and guides your activities towards understanding those longings.

Overflow Attitude: Embracing the conviction that there is enough for everybody and praising the outcome of others cultivates a mentality of joint effort and participation. Rather than seeing others as rivalry, you view them as possible partners and

Teammates, opening entryways for commonly advantageous open doors.

Making A roused Move: Creating overflow cognizance includes something beyond certain reasoning. It requires making a roused move toward your objectives. By adjusting your considerations, convictions, and activities, you set out energy and draw in open doors that help your vision of overflow.

Relinquishing Viewpoint that everything is limited: Delivering restricting convictions, fears, and shortage-based speculation designs is vital for creating overflow awareness. Perceive that shortage Believing is an educated way of behaving that can be untaught, and intentionally decide to supplant it with contemplations and convictions that help overflow.

By intentionally developing an overflow cognizance, you make an outlook that is responsive to riches, achievement, and satisfaction. This change in mentality permits you to perceive and immediately jump all over chances, settle on sure

Choices, and make moves that line up with your vision of enduring thriving.

Rehearsing Appreciation and Energy

Rehearsing appreciation and energy includes taking on a mentality and day-to-day propensities that emphasize valuing the positive parts of life and developing a feeling of appreciation for what we have. It includes recognizing and being appreciative of the favors, open doors, and, surprisingly, the little delights that come in our direction.

Appreciation is tied in with moving our consideration away from what might be missing or testing in our lives and on second thought perceiving the overflow and goodness that exists. It is a method for developing an uplifting perspective and tracking down satisfaction and satisfaction right now.

Rehearsing appreciation can be as straightforward as taking a couple of seconds every day to consider and communicate appreciation for the things we frequently underestimate, like our well-being, connections, achievements, or even the

Magnificence of nature. It includes being careful and present, permitting ourselves to experience and enjoy the positive parts of our lives genuinely.

By routinely recognizing and offering thanks, we train our brains to zero in on the positive parts of life, which can significantly affect our general prosperity. It can assist with diminishing pressure, working on our mindset, and improving our connections. Appreciation likewise assists us with creating versatility and a more noteworthy feeling of confidence, empowering us to explore difficulties with a more good and engaged mentality.

Notwithstanding appreciation, rehearsing energy includes deliberately deciding to take on a hopeful and confident demeanor toward life. It implies reevaluating negative circumstances or misfortunes as any open doors for development and learning. Positive reasoning can assist us with moving toward difficulties with a critical thinking outlook and see misfortunes as transitory as opposed to super durable.

Rehearsing appreciation and energy isn't tied in with denying or stifling gloomy feelings or troubles, yet rather about moving our viewpoint and zeroing in on the good parts of our lives. It is an integral asset for developing delight, flexibility, and a more prominent feeling of general prosperity.

Chapter 4

Dominating Establishing a strong financial foundation Procedures

Dominating and establishing strong financial foundation systems alludes to fostering the information and abilities important to develop and deal with your monetary assets. It includes embracing shrewd practices and going with informed choices to create financial momentum over the long haul. Here is an improved clarification of dominating and establishing strong financial foundation techniques:

Saving and Contributing for Long Haul Development: Saving alludes to saving a part of your pay consistently while putting includes placing your set aside cash into resources that can fill in esteem over the long haul. By understanding different venture choices like stocks, securities, land, or shared reserves, you can pursue informed choices on where to put away your cash to boost returns and accomplish long-haul monetary objectives.

Building Numerous Floods of Pay: Depending entirely on a solitary pay source can restrict your monetary development. Dominating establishing financial stability methodologies includes differentiating your pay by investigating extra wellsprings of income. This could incorporate beginning a side business, putting resources into pay creating resources, or chasing after open doors for recurring, automated revenue, for example, investment properties or profit-paying stocks.

Utilizing Open Doors: Hazard versus Reward: Understanding the idea of chance and prize is significant in establishing financial stability. Dominating this system includes recognizing and surveying valuable open doors that have the potential for critical returns. It requires cautious assessment of potential dangers related to speculation or undertaking, as well as gauging them against the possible prizes. By adjusting hazard and prize, you can pursue informed choices that line up with your monetary objectives.

It's critical to take note that dominating growing substantial financial foundation techniques likewise includes nonstop getting the hang of, remaining Refreshed on monetary patterns, and looking for direction from experts if necessary. Every individual's growing a substantial financial foundation venture is interesting, and the methodologies utilized may shift in light of individual conditions, risk resistance, and objectives.

Saving and Contributing to Long haul Development

Saving and contributing for long-haul development includes saving cash and giving it something to do in different monetary instruments determined to expand its worth over the long run. A technique assists people with creating financial momentum and accomplishing their monetary objectives later on.

Saving alludes to saving a part of your pay consistently and keeping it in a safe and effectively open record, for example, an investment account or a currency market account. Saving is commonly finished to make a secret stash, cover momentary Costs, or collect assets for explicit objectives like purchasing a house or going on a getaway. Saving is Pivotal as it gives a monetary pad and guarantees steadiness in the present.

Effective financial planning, then again, includes placing your cash into resources or venture vehicles that can fill in esteem over the long run. Not at all like saving, contributing involves taking in some capacity of chance in return for the amazing chance to procure better yields. Instances of normal venture choices incorporate stocks, securities, common assets, land, and trade exchanged reserves (ETFs).

Long-haul development contributing stresses effective financial planning with a period skyline of quite a while or even many years. The thought is to outfit the force of compounding, where the profits produced from ventures are reinvested, prompting remarkable development after some time. By remaining contributed as long as possible, financial backers might profit from market rises and brave market slumps, which will generally be transitory.

The vital standard behind long-haul development contributing is expansion. It includes spreading your Speculations across various resource classes and areas to diminish risk. Enhancement safeguards Against the expected adverse consequence of any single speculation and improves the probability of catching learning experiences in various regions of the market.

While saving and contributing for long-haul development, it's critical to lay out clear monetary objectives, lay out a financial plan, and designate a part of your pay explicitly for money management. Customary commitments to your venture portfolio, like through robotized month-to-month stores, can assist you with exploiting mitigating risk, which smooths out the effect of momentary market variances.

While effective financial planning for long-haul development offers the potential for better yields, it's fundamental to painstakingly assess your gamble resistance, lead examination, and look for proficient counsel if necessary. Figuring out the essentials of money management, being patient, and remaining focused on your drawn-out monetary arrangement can add to accomplishing enduring development and monetary flourishing.

Building Numerous Surges of Pay

Building numerous surges of pay alludes to the act of making different wellsprings of income or revenue streams as opposed to depending entirely on a solitary source, like compensation from a task. The thought behind this approach is to expand your pay sources, which can give more noteworthy monetary security and increment you're generally speaking acquiring potential.

Here is an improved clarification of building various floods of pay:

Enhancing Pay Sources: Rather than depending entirely on one work or undertaking, you investigate extra ways of producing pay. This can include chasing after various open doors all the while or bit by bit adding new revenue streams over the long haul.

Sorts of Revenue Sources: Numerous surges of pay can emerge out of different sources, for example,

Work Pay: Your essential work or profession that gives a normal check.
Side gigs: Seasonal positions, independent work, or private ventures that you take part in beyond your essential work.
Speculations: Acquiring pay from interests in stocks, bonds, land, or other monetary instruments.

Rental Pay: Bring in cash from properties you own and lease.

Sovereignties: Profit from innovative works, like books, music, or workmanship.

Recurring, automated revenue: Income produced from resources or speculations that require negligible exertion or time, like profits, interest, or online organizations.

Advantages of Various Revenue Sources: Building numerous floods of pay offers a few benefits, including:

Monetary Dependability: Assuming one pay source vacillates or is lost, you have different sources to depend on, diminishing the gamble of monetary difficulty.

Expanded Procuring Potential: By differentiating your pay, you have the valuable chance to procure more generally than you would with a solitary pay source.

Adaptability and Opportunity: Having numerous revenue streams can give greater adaptability in dealing with your time, permitting you to seek after different interests or invest energy with family.

Abundance Creation: Broadening your revenue streams can assist you with gathering abundance quicker by utilizing different roads for acquiring and money management.

Building Numerous Surges of Pay: To assemble various revenue sources, you might have to:

Recognize Potential open doors: Exploration and investigate different pay-producing roads that line up with your abilities, interests, and assets.

Secure New Abilities: Acquire new abilities or improve existing ones to seek extra revenue streams.

Make a move: Begin little and steadily fabricate every revenue stream over the long run, zeroing in on economical and versatile sources.

Oversee and Develop: Consistently screen and deal with your revenue sources, changing systems on a case-by-case basis to expand their true capacity.

Keep in mind, fabricating different floods of pay requires exertion, devotion, and an eagerness to investigate new open doors. It can give monetary Security, upgrade your acquiring potential, and add to long-haul abundance creation.

Utilizing Open Doors: Hazard versus Reward

Utilizing open doors includes surveying and exploiting circumstances that can yield positive results or rewards. Notwithstanding, it is essential to comprehend that each open door accompanies a specific degree of chance. The idea of chance versus reward alludes to the compromise between the likely advantages or gains of an open door and the expected adverse results or misfortunes.

Whenever you influence open doors, you consider the likely rewards or advantages that can be accomplished. This could incorporate monetary profits, professional successes, self-awareness, or other wanted results. The thought is to recognize amazing open doors that line up with your objectives and can push you toward enduring success.

In any case, it's essential to likewise assess the related dangers. Dangers can incorporate the chance of disappointment, monetary misfortunes, time and exertion used, or possible adverse consequences on Different aspects of your life. Via cautiously evaluating the dangers implied, you can settle on informed conclusions about which amazing open doors merit going after and which may not be reasonable for your conditions.

The way to successfully utilize open doors is to track down a harmony between hazard and prize. It includes leading careful examination, gathering data, and going with determined choices given the expected advantages and dangers implied. This doesn't mean keeping away from all dangers, yet rather understanding and overseeing them in a manner that lines up with your gamble resilience and generally speaking objectives.

Eventually, by utilizing open doors with a cautious evaluation of hazard versus reward, you can build your possibilities of making progress, development, and enduring thriving while at the same time limiting expected adverse results.

Chapter 5

Embracing Monetary Discipline

Embracing monetary discipline alludes to taking on a bunch of propensities and ways of behaving that advance dependable and careful administration of your monetary assets. It includes coming to cognizant conclusions about spending, saving, and money management, with an emphasis on long-haul monetary objectives and strength. Here is an improved clarification of embracing monetary discipline:

Planning and Overseeing Costs: Monetary discipline begins with making a financial plan that frames your pay and costs. By following your spending and guaranteeing that it lines up with your monetary objectives, you can make informed decisions about where your cash proceeds to stay away from superfluous or indiscreet buys.

Obligation The Board and End: Monetary discipline incorporates effectively overseeing and paying off past commitments. It includes making ordinary Installments on time, focusing on exorbitant interest

Obligations, and trying not to assume new obligations except if important. By paying off past commitments, you can let loose more assets for saving and effective financial planning.

Saving and Financial Planning: Monetary discipline stresses the significance of setting aside cash routinely and reliably. It includes saving a part of your pay for crises, future costs, and long-haul objectives. Furthermore, it supports effective money management of your investment funds shrewdly to create possible development and create financial well-being after some time.

Computerizing Growing a strong financial foundation Propensities: Monetary discipline frequently includes mechanizing specific monetary errands to make them simpler and more reliable. For instance, setting up programmed moves to reserve funds or venture accounts guarantees that a piece of your pay is saved or contributed before you get an opportunity to spend it.

Deferred Satisfaction: Embracing monetary discipline requires rehearsing postponed delight. Rather than yielding to indiscreet buys, it includes Assessing the drawn-out worth and effect of your monetary choices. This mentality assists you with focusing on your monetary objectives over transient longings, at last prompting better monetary results.

Adhering to an Arrangement: Monetary discipline includes making a monetary arrangement and adhering to it. This incorporates routinely exploring and changing your objectives, observing your headway, and rolling out essential improvements to keep focused.

By embracing monetary discipline, you can deal with your funds, lessen monetary pressure, and work towards accomplishing long-haul monetary soundness and flourishing. It enables you to pursue deliberate decisions that line up with your qualities and objectives, eventually prompting a safer and more satisfying monetary future.

Planning and Overseeing Costs

Planning and overseeing costs is the most common way of arranging and controlling how you spend your cash to guarantee that you meet your monetary objectives and live within your means. It includes following your pay and costs, settling on insightful

Conclusions about your spending, and focusing on your monetary necessities and needs.

Here is a straightforward clarification of planning and overseeing costs:

Following Pay: Start by understanding how much cash you acquire every month from all sources, like your compensation, independent work, or speculations. This is your pay.

Sorting Costs: Make a rundown of all your normal costs, like lease/contract, utilities, food, transportation, obligation installments, diversion, and reserve funds. Order each cost to get an unmistakable comprehension of where your cash is going.

Separating Necessities and Needs: Separate between your fundamental requirements and optional needs. Needs are things you should need to live, similar to food and asylum, while needs are things you want yet can live without, such as eating out or purchasing new devices.

Laying out Monetary Objectives: Decide your present moment and long-haul monetary objectives. These objectives can incorporate putting something aside for crises, taking care of obligations, putting Something aside for retirement, or purchasing a house. Having clear objectives assists you with focusing on your spending.

Making a Financial Plan: Given your pay and costs, make a spending plan that distributes your cash towards various classes. Begin by covering your necessities and afterward designate assets for your needs and investment funds objectives. Ensure your absolute costs don't surpass your pay.

Checking and Changing: Consistently track your costs and contrast them with your financial plan. This will assist you with distinguishing regions where you might be overspending or regions where you can save more. Change your spending plan likewise to line up with your monetary objectives.

Going with Informed Choices: While settling on buying choices, think about your spending plan and needs. Inquire as to whether the cost is fundamental, if there are less expensive other options, or on the

Other hand if it very well may be deferred. Being aware of your ways of managing money can assist you with pursuing informed decisions.

Building a Backup stash: Designate a part of your pay to a rainy day account to cover startling costs or monetary difficulties. This asset goes about as a well-being net and keeps you from venturing into the red when crises emerge.

Looking for Ways Of saving: Search for chances to set aside cash. This can remember scaling back for optional costs, tracking down additional reasonable other options, arranging bills, or looking for limits and coupons.

Investigating and Changing Consistently: Audit your spending plan occasionally to guarantee it mirrors what is happening and its objectives. Change it on a case-by-case basis to oblige any pay changes or changes in your needs.

By planning and overseeing costs really, you can deal with your funds, lessen monetary pressure, and work towards accomplishing your monetary objectives.

Obligation The board and End

Obligation the board and end allude to methodologies and practices focused on really Overseeing and in the long run disposing of obligation. The obligation is cash acquired from a bank or lender that should be reimbursed over a predetermined period, regularly with a premium. While obligation can be a valuable device for accomplishing monetary objectives or taking care of crises, the extreme or blundered obligation can become oppressive and upset one's monetary prosperity.

Obligations The board includes sorting out and directing your obligations to guarantee ideal installments and limit monetary strain. It incorporates different procedures, for example,

Planning: Make a far-reaching spending plan that records your pay, costs, and obligation installments. This permits you to designate a piece of your pay towards reimbursing obligations every month.

Focusing on Obligation Installments: Assessing your obligations and recognizing the ones with the most elevated loan fees or those causing the most monetary strain. By focusing on these obligations, you can zero in on taking care of them first while making the least installments on others.

Haggling with Loan bosses: Reaching your lenders to examine possible choices for decreasing financing costs, changing reimbursement terms, or laying out a more sensible installment plan. Numerous leaders will work with borrowers to track down commonly useful arrangements.

Merging Obligation: Joining numerous obligations into a solitary credit or acknowledgment represent better terms, for example, a lower loan fee or a more drawn-out reimbursement period. Obligation union improves the reimbursement interaction and can assist with decreasing generally speaking interest costs.

Obligation disposal expects to kill exceptional obligations, giving independence from the rat race and an inward feeling of harmony. It includes techniques, for example,

Snowball Strategy: Beginning by taking care of the littlest obligation first while making the least installments on different obligations. When the littlest obligation is paid off, the cash recently designated to it is then coordinated towards the Following littlest obligation. This approach gives a feeling of achievement and inspiration as obligations are step by step disposed of.

Torrential slide Technique: Focusing on obligation reimbursement given loan fees. Beginning with the obligation conveying the most noteworthy financing cost and taking care of it first, then moving to the following most elevated loan fee obligation. This technique sets aside more cash in revenue installments over the long haul.

Expanding Installments: Dispensing extra assets, like bonuses or additional pay, towards obligation reimbursement. By making bigger installments, you can speed up the obligation disposal process and decrease the general interest paid.

Looking for Proficient Assistance: at times, looking for help from credit directing offices or monetary counselors can give direction and back in fostering a customized obligation end plan.

Generally speaking, the obligation of the board and end include carrying out procedures to successfully oversee and pay off past commitments, assisting People with recovering control of their funds and working towards an obligation-free future. It requires discipline, responsibility, and a proactive way to deal with monetary preparation and planning.

Robotizing Establishing financial stability Propensities

Robotizing establishing a strong financial foundation propensities alludes to setting up frameworks and cycles that naturally add to your monetary development and accomplishment without requiring steady exertion or cognizant navigation. It includes coming up with schedules and carrying out methodologies that smooth out your monetary activities, making it simpler to save, contribute, and create financial momentum over the long run.

Here is a straightforward comprehension clarification of mechanizing establishing financial stability propensities:

Programmed Reserve funds: One ward building propensity is setting up programmed moves from your check or ledger to a devoted investment funds or venture account. Via computerizing this cycle, a part of your pay is naturally saved without you Having to physically move the cash each time. This guarantees predictable reserve funds and assists you with building a monetary pad or venture portfolio after some time.

Robotized Bill Installments: Mechanizing bill installments guarantees that your monetary commitments, like lease, utilities, and advance reimbursements, are paid on time. This dispenses with the gamble of late expenses or punishments and keeps a decent FICO rating, which is essential for long-haul monetary dependability.

Speculation Robotization: Contributing consistently is a critical part of establishing a strong financial foundation. Mechanizing your speculations can include setting up repeating commitments to

Retirement accounts like a 401(k) or IRA, or utilizing robo-counsels or venture applications that naturally dispense reserves in light of your inclinations and change resilience. This approach permits your speculations to develop over the long haul, exploiting accumulate revenue and market vacillations.

Cost Following and Planning: Robotizing cost following through applications or programming assists you with remaining mindful of your ways of managing money and guarantees that you are adhering to a spending plan. By synchronizing your records and ordering exchanges consequently, you can undoubtedly investigate where your cash is proceeding to make fundamental acclimations to adjust your spending to your monetary objectives.

Programmed Obligation Reimbursement: On the off chance that you have obligations, robotizing your obligation installments can assist you with keeping focused and staying away from late installments. Setting up programmed installments for Visas, understudy loans, or home loans guarantees that the base required installment is made immediately every

Month, diminishing the gamble of collecting extra interest or punishments.

Via computerizing growing long-term financial stability propensities, you make a design that energizes predictable monetary activities and eliminates the dependence on resolve or steady navigation. This approach assists you with creating financial stability slowly and easily, making it simpler to accomplish your drawn-out monetary objectives.

Chapter 6

Utilizing the Force of Organizations and Connections

Utilizing the force of organizations and connections includes using the associations and cooperations you have with others to improve your own proficient development. It perceives that individuals you know and the connections you construct can assume a critical part in assisting you with accomplishing your objectives and advancing in different parts of life.

By effectively captivating your organization and sustaining connections, you can help in more than one way. Here is an improved clarification of how it functions:

Admittance to Open Doors: Your organization comprises people from assorted foundations, callings, and encounters. By taking advantage of this organization, you get a great many open doors like employment opportunities, business associations, Cooperative tasks, and growth opportunities. These

Potential open doors may not be promptly accessible to you in any case.

Information and Data Sharing: Every individual in your organization has novel information, abilities, and viewpoints. By cultivating connections and participating in significant discussions, you can trade thoughts, bits of knowledge, and data. This sharing of information can assist you with acquiring new points of view, gaining from others' encounters, and remaining refreshed with industry patterns.

Backing and Direction: Organizations and connections offer a helpful framework. When confronted with difficulties or vulnerabilities, you can go to your confided-in associations for exhortation, direction, and consistent encouragement. They can offer significant experiences, share their aptitude, and give the consolation to assist you with exploring tough spots or settling on significant choices.

Coordinated effort and Cooperative energy: Organizations are rich ground for a coordinated effort. By interfacing with similar people or those With corresponding abilities, you can frame

Associations or groups to chip away at ventures or drives. Cooperative endeavors frequently lead to collaboration, where the joined endeavors of people yield more noteworthy outcomes than what every individual could accomplish alone.

Self-improvement and Advancement: Associating with assorted people permit you to expand your perspectives and extend your insight. Participating in conversations, going to occasions, or taking part in systems administration exercises opens you to alternate points of view, challenges your presumptions, and animates self-awareness. You can acquire new abilities, gain certainty, and improve your correspondence and relational capacities.

To use the force of organizations and connections really, it's urgent to be proactive, authentic, and respond to the help you get. Effectively draw in your associations, show interest in their undertakings, and proposition your help when required. Constructing and keeping up major areas of strength takes time and exertion, however, the advantages can be critical in both individual and expert settings.

Building Areas of Strength for a Framework

Building areas of strength for a framework alludes to the most common way of developing an organization of people who give consolation, direction, and help with different parts of your life. This organization normally comprises individuals who have confidence in your objectives, offer consistent reassurance, and give commonsense assistance when required.

Here is a straightforward grasping clarification of building areas of strength for a framework:

Recognize your requirements: Decide the aspects of your life where you could profit from help. It very well may be private, proficient, instructive, or some other perspective.

Perceive the sorts of help: Comprehend the various kinds of help you might require. This can incorporate consistent reassurance, for example, somebody who tunes in and offers sympathy, or commonsense help, similar to somebody who Furnishes exhortation or helps you with explicit undertakings.

Evaluate existing connections: Consider individuals currently in your life who might be important to your emotionally supportive network. Companions, relatives, partners, guides, or local area individuals can all assume a part.

Search out new associations: Effectively look for valuable chances to grow your emotionally supportive network. This can include joining clubs, going to systems administration occasions, taking part in web-based networks, or searching out tutors or mentors in your field of interest.

Sustain connections: Whenever you've distinguished people who can be essential for your emotionally supportive network, put time and exertion into the building and keeping up with these connections. Show certified interest in their lives, be a decent audience, and give support as a trade-off whenever the situation allows.

Impart your requirements: Be transparent about your objectives, goals, and difficulties with your Encouraging group of people. Convey what sort of help you want and how they can help you.

Offer help to other people: areas of strength for a framework are based on correspondence. Offer help, guidance, and support to others in your organization. By being there for other people, you reinforce the obligations of trust and establish a steady climate.

Consistently check in Stay in contact with your emotionally supportive network consistently. This can include getting together for espresso, planning calls, or remaining associated through virtual entertainment. Customary registrations assist with keeping up with the strength and adequacy of your emotionally supportive network.

Keep in mind, constructing areas of strength for a framework is a ceaseless cycle that requires exertion and sustaining. By encircling yourself with positive and steady people, you can improve your self-improvement, conquer difficulties, and accomplish your objectives effortlessly.

Working together and Systems administration for Progress

Working together and organizing are fundamental components for making progress in different everyday issues, including business, professional Success, and self-improvement. Here is a basic comprehension clarification of working together and organizing for progress:

Working together:
Cooperation includes cooperating with others toward a shared objective or reason. It goes past individual endeavors and energizes the pooling of assets, abilities, and information to accomplish improved results. In a cooperative climate, people or gatherings share their mastery, thoughts, and encounters to make creative arrangements, increment efficiency, and achieve undertakings all the more proficiently. Joint effort frequently underlines open correspondence, trust, and a readiness to think twice about helping out others. By working together, people can use the qualities of each colleague and accomplish results that would be troublesome or difficult to achieve alone.

Organizing:

Organizing alludes to the most common way of building and sustaining associations with individuals who can offer significant help, data, and potentially open doors. It includes effectively captivating others, both inside and beyond your nearby circles, To lay out associations and trade assets. Systems administration can happen through different channels, like proficient occasions, parties, online stages, and industry-explicit networks. By extending your organization, you get assorted points of view, information, and possible colleagues or guides who can assist you with accomplishing your objectives. Successful systems administration includes certified correspondence, undivided attention, shared help, and an eagerness to offer help to other people. It is a two-way road where the two players benefit from the relationship.

Working together and organizing for progress:
Teaming up and organizing work connected at the hip to improve progress in different regions. At the point when you team up with others, you tap into their skill and assets, profiting from an aggregate exertion that can prompt more noteworthy accomplishments. By systems administration, you Interface with people who can offer direction,

acquaint you with amazing open doors, and give significant experiences or counsel. The cooperative attitude permits you to settle on some shared interest with others, assemble trust, and cultivate commonly valuable connections through systems Administration. Together, these practices can open ways to new associations, grow your insight base, and increment your perce inside your field or the local area, at last prompting expanded outcomes in your undertakings.

Tutors and Good Examples: Gaining from the Best

Tutors and good examples assume an essential part in our proficient improvement by offering direction, motivation, and backing. Here is a basic comprehension clarification of tutors and good examples:

Tutors: Coaches are capable people who give direction, counsel, and back to somebody who is less capable or learned in a specific field or everyday issue. They offer their aptitude, share their Encounters, and give significant experiences to help mentees develop, learn, and accomplish their objectives. Guides can be found in different regions like professions, scholastics, business, and self-improvement, and the sky is the limit from there. They go about as confided-in guides, giving Productive criticism, helping mentees explore difficulties, and offering support en route. A guide-mentee relationship is normally founded on Common regard, trust, and an eagerness to learn and develop.

Good examples: Good examples are people who rouse and act as guides to other people. They epitomize characteristics, values, and accomplishments that others try to copy. Good examples can be found in different everyday issues, including sports, diversion, business, administration, and local area administration, and the sky is the limit from there. They exhibit greatness, honesty, constancy, and other advantageous attributes that make them stick out. By noticing and gaining from good examples, people can acquire motivation, inspiration, and an internal compass. Good examples can impact conduct, perspectives, and decisions, Filling in as a wellspring of motivation for self-improvement and accomplishment.

Gaining from the Best: The two tutors and good examples give important chances to gain from the people who have proactively made progress or have succeeded in their separate fields. By noticing and Concentrating on their activities, perspectives, and systems, we can acquire experiences that have added to their prosperity. Gaining from the best includes Distinguishing and grasping the characteristics, abilities, and propensities that have impelled them forward. It likewise includes looking for direction and exhortation from coaches who can offer customized help and information intended for our objectives and goals. By gaining from all that, we can speed up our development, stay away from normal entanglements, and gain significant information and abilities that can assist us with making progress in our own lives.

In outline, tutors and good examples are fundamental wellsprings of direction and motivation. Tutors offer customized help and guidance, while good examples offer motivation and act as instances of greatness. Gaining from the best Includes noticing, examining, and looking for direction from these people to speed up our very own proficient turn of events.

Chapter 7

Exploring Difficulties and Defeating Snags

Exploring provokes and beating hindrances alludes to the course of actually managing tough spots or road obstructions that might emerge on your way to Progress. It includes creating techniques, mentality, and versatility to beat obstacles and push ahead.

When confronted with difficulties, it's crucial to approach them with a positive and arrangement-situated mentality. Rather than survey hindrances as impossible obstructions, consider them to be amazing open doors for development and learning. By embracing difficulties, you can foster new abilities, gain important encounters, and become better prepared to deal with future hindrances.

To explore difficulties and conquer hindrances, think about the accompanying advances:

Distinguish the test: Perceive and characterize the particular issue or obstruction that you are Confronting. Understanding the idea of the test permits you to zero in on your endeavors on tracking down fitting arrangements.

Investigate and assemble data: Accumulate pertinent data and dissect what is going on to acquire a complete comprehension of the test. This might include investigating, looking for exhortation from Specialists or coaches, or gaining from other people who have confronted comparable impediments.

Separate it: Separate the test into more modest, sensible assignments or objectives. This makes it less overpowering and permits you to handle each viewpoint in turn, expanding your odds of coming out on top.

Foster an arrangement: Make a thoroughly examined strategy. Recognize explicit advances and procedures that will assist you with tending to the test. Set practical cutoff times and achievements to keep tabs on your development.

Adjust and change: Be ready to adjust your arrangement depending on the situation. Difficulties might require adaptability and the capacity to Change your methodology given new data or unexpected conditions. Remain receptive and attempt various arrangements if fundamental.

Look for help: Make it a point to request help or look for help from others. This could include looking for exhortation from tutors, teaming up with partners, or contacting a strong organization. In Some cases, new viewpoints and directions can give significant bits of knowledge and arrangements.

Keep a positive mentality: Keep an uplifting perspective in the meantime. Difficulties can be intellectually and genuinely depleting, yet remaining hopeful and zeroed in on arrangements will assist you with remaining persuaded and versatile. Celebrate little wins en route to help your certainty and force.

Gain from misfortunes: Difficulties and disappointments are unavoidable in any excursion. Rather than being deterred by them, view mishaps as learning valuable open doors. Investigate what turned out badly, separate important illustrations, and change your methodology as needs be. Use Mishaps as venturing stones toward future achievement.

By following these means and taking on a proactive and versatile mentality, you can explore difficulties and conquer impediments on your way to progress. Keep in mind, challenges are much of the time open doors in masks, and beating them can prompt Self-awareness, expanded versatility, and eventually, accomplishing your objectives.

Embracing Disappointment as a Learning An open door

Embracing disappointment as a learning opportunity implies perceiving that disappointments and difficulties are not extremely durable deterrents but rather significant encounters that can add to individual and expert development. Rather than survey disappointment as something to be embarrassed about or stayed away from, it is viewed as a venturing stone towards progress.

Whenever we embrace disappointment as a learning and a valuable open door, we shift our mentality to Zero in on the examples and bits of knowledge that can be acquired from the experience. As opposed to harping on the negative parts of disappointment, we effectively try to comprehend what turned out badly, why it worked out, and what we can do another way later on.

One of the vital parts of embracing disappointment is reevaluating our point of view on botches. Rather than seeing them as marks of ineptitude or Deficiency, we view them as normal and important pieces of the growing experience. By reevaluating disappointment as a venturing stone toward progress, we can move toward it with interest and receptiveness, prepared to extricate significant illustrations from the experience.

Embracing disappointment as a learning opportunity likewise includes taking on a development mentality. This attitude perceives that capacities and abilities can be created through commitment, exertion, and tirelessness. Instead of survey disappointment as proof of fixed limits, a development outlook considers it to be an opportunity to procure new information, foster versatility, and refine techniques for progress.
By embracing disappointment as a learning and open door, we become stronger and more versatile.

We figure out how to dissect our mix-ups equitably, distinguish regions for development, and make important acclimations to our methodology. Disappointment turns into an impetus for self-improvement, empowering us to refine our abilities, foster new methodologies, and eventually Jncrement our odds of coming out on top in later undertakings.

In general, embracing disappointment as a learning opportunity includes a change in mentality, where disappointment is viewed as an important educator as opposed to an indication of a rout. It permits us to separate illustrations, foster versatility, and ceaselessly work on ourselves, eventually prompting more noteworthy accomplishments and enduring achievements.

Beating Dread and Going Ahead with Reasonable Courses of Action

Defeating Dread and Going Ahead with Well balanced Plans of Action

Dread is a characteristic human feeling that frequently keeps us from facing challenges and venturing beyond our usual ranges of familiarity. It can keep us away from seeking open doors that could prompt individual and monetary development. Notwithstanding, beating dread and figuring out how to go ahead with reasonable courses of action is fundamental for accomplishing enduring thriving.

To conquer dread, it's essential to comprehend that dread is many times given silly considerations and restricting convictions. It is in many cases established in the feeling of dread toward disappointment, dismissal, or the unexplored world. Perceiving and testing these contemplations is the most important phase in defeating dread.

Going ahead with reasonable courses of action includes pursuing informed choices after cautiously surveying the expected advantages and disadvantages. It's not necessary to focus on being wild or incautious but instead on considering the expected results and gauging them in contrast to the possible prizes.

Here are some vital stages to conquer dread and proceed with reasonable plans of action:

Distinguish the trepidation: Perceive the particular apprehension that is keeping you down. Is it the anxiety toward disappointment, the apprehension about monetary misfortune, or the anxiety toward what others could think? Understanding the main driver of your apprehension will assist you with tending to it more actually.

Assemble data: Instruct yourself about the circumstance or opportunity you are thinking about. Examination and assemble significant data to go with an educated choice. Information and understanding can assist with mitigating dread and increment certainty.

Assess the possible dangers and prizes: Evaluate the expected dangers and prizes related to the choice or opportunity. Think about both the present moment and long-haul suggestions. By gauging the possible results, you can pursue an additional sane and determined choice.

Plan and get ready: Foster a thoroughly examined plan and set yourself up for the expected difficulties and hindrances that might emerge. Having a strong arrangement set up can give a feeling that everything is good and certain, decreasing trepidation.

Begin little and gather speed: Making little strides toward your objective can assist you with building certainty and defeat dread continuously. Begin with more modest dangers and step by step increment the degree of challenge as you acquire insight and certainty.

Embrace disappointment as a learning a valuable open door: Comprehend that disappointment is a characteristic piece of the educational experience. Rather than allowing inability to deter you, view it as a chance to learn, develop, and move along. Every mishap can give important illustrations that can drive you forward.

Look for help and direction: Encircle yourself with strong people who put stock in your true capacity and urge you to go ahead with well-balanced plans of action. Look for direction from tutors or Specialists who have insight into the areas you are wandering into. Their bits of knowledge and counsel can assist you with exploring difficulties all the more.

By defeating dread and going ahead with potentially dangerous courses of action, you extend your usual range of familiarity, free yourself up to new open doors, and increment your possibilities of accomplishing enduring success. Keep in mind, development and achievement frequently lie just past the limits of dread.

Steadiness and Versatility: Remaining on the Way to Riches

Tirelessness and flexibility are two significant characteristics that can assist people with remaining on the way to abundance.

Steadiness alludes to the capacity to endure not set in stone in that frame of mind of difficulties, mishaps, or deterrents. It implies not surrendering effectively and remaining focused on accomplishing your objectives, in any event, when the excursion Becomes troublesome. With regards to establishing financial stability, the determination includes keeping fixed on your monetary targets, despite any mishaps or impermanent disappointments you might experience en route. It requires keeping a drawn-out mentality and having the assurance to continue to push forward, in any event, when things don't go as expected.

Strength, then again, is the ability to return and recuperate rapidly from misfortune or troublesome conditions. It includes having the psychological and Close-to-home solidarity to adjust and answer decidedly to difficulties, instead of being overpowered by them. Chasing abundance, and strength is significant because monetary achievement frequently accompanies its reasonable portion of promising and less promising times. It implies having the option to gain from disappointments, change your systems when required, and keep an uplifting perspective even notwithstanding monetary mishaps or financial vulnerabilities.

Both steadiness and versatility are entwined and integral. Diligence assists you with keeping up with Concentration and assurance, while strength empowers you to quickly return and adjust when confronted with deterrents or mishaps. Together, these characteristics can enable you to remain on the way to abundance by enduring difficulties, gaining from disappointments, and staying resolute in your quest for monetary achievement. They give the strength and outlook expected to conquer troubles, remain propelled, and eventually accomplish enduring thriving.

Chapter 8

Leaving an Enduring Inheritance

Passing on an enduring inheritance alludes to the demonstration of making a positive and persevering influence that keeps on helping others even after you're at this point not present. It includes making significant commitments and impacting the existence of people in the future, whether through your activities, accomplishments, values, or generous undertakings.

Leaving an enduring inheritance is tied in with abandoning something that affects the world or individuals around you. It can take different structures, for example,

Affecting others: One method for leaving an enduring heritage is by decidedly impacting the existences of others. This can be accomplished through coaching, educating, moving, or offering help to people or networks. By conferring your insight, shrewdness, and values, you add to the individual and expert development of others.

Making change: Leaving an enduring heritage can include having an effect in a specific region or tending to cultural difficulties. It might involve supporting a reason, pushing for civil rights, or pursuing ecological supportability. By devoting your endeavors to making positive change, you make an imprint that benefits people in the future.

Generosity and offering in return: One more method for leaving an enduring heritage is through magnanimity and beneficent demonstrations. By giving assets, time, or mastery to associations or causes that line up with your qualities, you can have an enduring effect on the existence of those out of luck. Altruistic undertakings frequently center around supporting instruction, medical care, destitution easing, or social drives.

Sharing information and shrewdness: Moving information and intelligence is a strong method for leaving an enduring inheritance. This can be achieved through composing books, making instructive materials, archiving encounters, or passing down customs and values to people in the future. By sharing your mastery and bits of Knowledge, you enable others to learn, develop, and have an effect.

Moving and persuading others: Leaving an enduring heritage can include being a wellspring of motivation and inspiration for other people. By carrying on with an existence of direction, strength, and assurance, you can motivate people around you to seek after their fantasies and yearnings. Your uplifting outlook and activities can make an expanding influence, rousing others to do great things.

Eventually, leaving an enduring inheritance is tied in with making a positive and enduring engraving on the world and individuals you experience. It is a method for guaranteeing that your impact and commitments keep on shaping the existences of others, making a superior future long after you're gone.

Charity and Offering in return

Generosity and offering back allude to the demonstration of willfully giving time, assets, or Cash to help other people or backing admirable missions. It is driven by a craving to have a constructive outcome on society and further develop the prosperity of others, frequently with an emphasis On tending to social, natural, or compassionate issues.

Magnanimity includes something beyond giving cash; it can likewise incorporate contributing mastery, abilities, or individual inclusion to achieve positive change. It is established in the conviction that people should utilize their assets and impact to help those out of luck and make a superior world.

Offering back can take different structures, like supporting philanthropic associations, noble causes, or local area drives. It might include financing instructive projects, medical care administrations, destitution-easing projects, ecological protection endeavors, or some other reason lined up with a singular's qualities and interests.

The demonstration of offering back helps the beneficiaries as well as gives individual satisfaction and fulfillment to the altruist. It permits people to interface with their networks, makes significant Connections, and add to the benefit of everyone. Besides, generosity can move others to reach out and make an expanding influence of positive change.

Altruism and offering back can be rehearsed by individuals from varying backgrounds, no matter what their monetary means. It is an amazing asset for advancing civil rights, balance, and supportable turn of events. Whether through little thoughtful gestures or huge-scope humanitarian undertakings, offering back is a fundamental part of building an empathetic and flourishing society.

Domain Arranging and Abundance Safeguarding

Domain Arranging

Domain arranging is the method involved with arranging the administration and dispersion of your resources after your demise. It includes going with significant choices regarding who will acquire your property, how it will be conveyed, and who will be answerable for completing your desires.

The critical parts of bequest arranging ordinarily include:

Will: An authoritative record that frames your desires for the circulation of your resources, designates an agent to deal with your home, and May incorporate guidelines for guardianship of minor kids if material.

Trusts: A trust is a legitimate plan where you move your resources for a legal administrator to oversee and circulate them as per your directions. Trusts can offer different advantages, for example, keeping away from probate, limiting domain burdens, and accommodating explicit circumstances or necessities of recipients.

General legal authority: This archive assigns somebody to follow up for your sake on monetary and legitimate issues if you become debilitated or unfit to simply decide.

Medical services Mandate or Living Will: These reports express your inclinations for clinical therapy and end-of-life care if you can't impart your desires.

Recipient Assignments: Naming recipients for retirement accounts, life coverage strategies, and different resources can guarantee a smooth exchange of those resources straightforwardly to the assigned people without going through probate.

Abundance Safeguarding

Abundance safeguarding alludes to the techniques and moves made to secure and keep up with the worth of your resources over the long run. It implies limiting dangers, advancing assessment productivity, and protecting your abundance for people in the future. A few normal strategies for abundance safeguarding include:

Enhancement: Spreading your ventures across various resource classes and areas can assist with lessening the gamble of misfortune because of the presentation of any single speculation.

Resource Security: Organizing your resources such that safeguards them from possible leasers or legitimate cases, like utilizing trusts or other lawful substances.

Charge Arranging: Using legitimate expense procedures to limit your duty risk and amplify your after-government forms on ventures.

Protection: Sufficient protection inclusion, including life coverage, risk protection, and property Protection, can shield your resources from surprising occasions and liabilities.

Progression Arranging: Fostering an arrangement for the smooth exchange of your resources and obligations to the future, limiting expected clashes, and guaranteeing coherence of your riches.

Abundance conservation procedures are frequently coordinated into bequests wanting to guarantee that your resources are effectively moved as well as secured and saved as long as possible. It's vital to work with experts, for example, bequest arranging lawyers and monetary guides to fit these techniques to your particular conditions and objectives.

Sharing Insight and Motivating Others

Sharing insight and moving others includes conferring information, bits of knowledge, and Encounters to help other people develop, learn, and make their progress. It is the demonstration of passing on important examples, directions, and points of view that can decidedly affect and engage others on their excursions.

At the point when we share astuteness, we draw upon our background, illustrations learned, and ability to give direction and back to other people. This can incorporate sharing useful exhortation, techniques for progress, and individual stories that exhibit versatility, beating snags, and accomplishing objectives. By sharing our insight, we can help other people keep away from normal entanglements, explore difficulties, and settle on informed choices.

Moving others goes past sharing information and includes propelling and empowering people to have faith in their true capacity and seek after their goals. Through our words, activities, and model, we can motivate others to think beyond practical boundaries, put forth aggressive objectives, and make a move to accomplish them. Moving others frequently includes being a good example, showing enthusiasm, assurance, and steadiness, and imparting a feeling of conviction and trust in others.
At the point when we share intelligence and rouse others, we add to a culture of learning, development, and backing. By lifting others and assisting them with fostering their abilities, information, and mentality, we make a gradually expanding influence Of positive change. It is a strong method for having an effect on the existences of others and adding to their proficient turn of events.

Eventually, sharing insight and rousing others is tied in with making a steady and elevating local area where people can gain from each other, become together, and accomplish their maximum capacity.

Conclusion

Releasing Your Full Growing a substantial financial foundation Potential" alludes to the method involved with taking advantage of and boosting your capacity to make riches and monetary overflow. It includes opening and using the abilities, information, assets, and attitude important to construct maintainable and enduring success.

To release your full growing strong financial foundation potential, you want to comprehend and foster a few key viewpoints:

Mindfulness: Gain a reasonable comprehension of your monetary objectives, values, qualities, and shortcomings. This information will assist you with adjusting your endeavors and assets in the best and most satisfying ways.

Outlook shift: Take on a positive and overflow-centered mentality. Recognize and defeat any restricting convictions or fears about cash and riches. Develop a mentality that embraces valuable open doors, proceeds with well-balanced plans of Action, and has confidence in your capacity to make and draw in riches.

Monetary training: Put resources into your monetary information and understanding. Find out about different growing long-term financial stability methodologies, for example, saving, money management, various revenue sources, and utilizing valuable open doors. Remain refreshed on monetary patterns and advancements to pursue informed choices.

Restrained activity: Foster-trained propensities and ways of behaving that help establish financial stability. This incorporates viable planning, overseeing costs, paying off past commitments, and computerizing growing long-term financial stability processes. Consistency and discipline in your monetary activities are fundamental for long-haul achievement.

Organization and connections: Construct areas of strength for strong and similar people. Encircle yourself with tutors, good examples, and friends who can give direction, motivation, and potentially Open doors. Team up with others to use aggregate information and assets.

Flexibility and versatility: Expect and embrace difficulties along your growing long-term financial stability venture. Foster versatility to conquer misfortunes, gain from disappointments and adjust your methodologies on a case-by-case basis. Diligence and flexibility are critical for remaining focused on your objectives.

Leaving a heritage: Consider the effect you need to make past your privately invested money. Investigate ways of rewarding your local area, support causes you to care about, and leave an enduring positive impact. Making a significant inheritance adds reason and satisfaction to your establishing long-term financial stability venture.

By releasing your full establishing long-term financial stability potential, you are engaging yourself to assume command over your monetary future, go with informed choices, and make enduring thriving for you and others. A cycle joins self-improvement, monetary information, restrained activity, and a mentality of overflow.